BODY OF WATER

ALSO BY JANET HAMILL

Lost Ceilings

Nostalgia of the Infinite

The Temple

Troublante

BODY OF WATER

Janet Hamill

BOWERY Books
BOWERY POETRY SERIES #6

YBK Publishers
New York

Body of Water
Copyright © 2008 by Janet Hamill

All rights reserved. No part of this work may be used or reproduced in any manner without permission in writing from the publisher, YBK Publishers, Inc., except in the case of brief quotations embodied in critical articles and reviews.

Please direct all inquiries to:
Editors
Bowery Books
310 Bowery
New York, NY 10012

Bowery Books   Bowery Voices Series
Editors Bob Holman and Marjorie Tesser

Cover photograph, Water Bearer Buenos Aires © 2006; Moving Clouds © 2003; Winged Horse The Palace of Music Barcelona © 2004; Glasgow Necropolis © 2006; St. Mungo's Cathedral Glasgow © 2006; La National Steel Guitar of Oliver Ray © 2003, Patti Smith.

Back cover author photograph by Fran O'Gorman

ISBN: 978-0-9800508-6-8

Library of Congress Control Number: 2008939192

Manufactured in the United States of America

Bowery Books are published in affiliation with
YBK Publishers, Inc.,
39 Crosby Street,
New York, NY 10013,
whose publisher, Otto Barz, is the inspiration for this series.
With thanks to Bill Adler.

Bowery Books is the imprint of Bowery Arts and Science, a non-profit cultural organization. We are grateful for the assistance we receive from individual donors, foundations and government arts agencies.

This publication is made possible with public funds from The New York State Council on the Arts, a state agency.

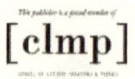

ACKNOWLEDGMENTS

Some of these poems have appeared in *Alchemy of the Word, Bowery Women: Poems, Calling All Poets, Deep Down: The New Sensual Writing by Women, Sweet Little Sixteen*, Big City Lit, Caprice, Café Review, City Lights Review, Contact II, For Immediate Release, Gallery Works, Heart Beats, Kansas Quarterly, #, Poetry Flash, Recluse, Telephone, and The World

Quoted material in "Out of the Blue," p. 5, Baudelaire, Charles, *Les Fleurs Du Mal*. Trans. Richard Howard. Boston: David R. Godine, 1982

Quoted material in "Land of the Great Image," p. 8, Gene Pitney, "He's a Rebel" January Music Corp., BMI

Photographs by Patti Smith

Water Bearer Buenos Aires
Moving Clouds
Winged Horse The Palace of Music Barcelona
Glasgow Necropolis
St. Mungo's Cathedral Glasgow
La National Steel Guitar of Oliver Ray

To the memory of my parents,
William and Loretta Hamill

CONTENTS

Body of Water   1
Nine Card Spread   2
The Green Harmonica   4
Out of the Blue   5
St. George and the Dragon   7
Land of the Great Image   8
Flying Nowhere   11
The Philosopher's Egg   14
Votive   15
Star Party   16
Seven Veils   18
Aria   21
Friendship with the Virgin   22
My Macumba   23
The Man with the Scarlet Kneebands   24
Sovereignty of the Clouds   27
Open Window   28
Moving Star   29
Spellbound   31
Boy Blue   33
A Thousand Years   34
Sleeping Gypsy   36
Insomnie   37
Tomb for Ophelia   39
Fan Motif at Noh Theatre   40
Requiem   41
Sea Fever   42
Phantom Vessel   43
Dark Skies   44
Door to Door   45

Altar Piece   47
Sacrifice End   50

HOMAGES

I, Fellini   54
Red Hills and Sky   60
Heathrow Sunflower   62
The Enigma of Buster Keaton   63
Blue Tango Shoes   67
K E R O U A C   68
Doom's Day Pie   70
Byron's Time Sheet   71

MOON MUSIC

1.   77
2.   78
3.   79
4.   81
5.   83
6.   85

Let night come on bells end the day
The days go by me still I stay....

- Apollinaire

BODY OF WATER

Standing by a body of water. Moving
or standing still. In the dark green depths
my soul finds its own level

Lost in a mirror of infinite margins. Ever
sounding. On and on. Perpetual arms pull me
under light's silver sheets. Tossed with wind
and waves. Where a coiled muscle gives up
a perfect word. I come with only a fever to offer
far from the dried carnations in summer's throat
and certain birds that pierce the air with agonizing
cries. I come to wash and be clean. To drown
in my immensity

Baptized by a spray of distant sky. In sympathetic
response. The surface repeats the hypnotic patterns
of my longing. Again and again. Swimming out
to the breaking pages before me. With only
a parched fountain to offer. Far from the sun's
entrenched lullaby of insect music and the worried
sleep that parts with a film of sweat and dust
I come to be carried away through the charitable
doors that open on the shore

Standing by a body of water. Moving
or standing still. In the dark green depths
my soul finds its own level

NINE CARD SPREAD

There's a deck of cards face down on the table

Will the night's apocalyptic starfish still swim in the stream
    circling the lady's waist?
Will her garden always yield pearls of jellied moon
    ripped from the side of florescent sharks?
Will her walls anchored in the sea floor uphold trellises
    laced with continuous light?

There's a deck of cards face down on the table

Will the lady find herself hanging upside down in a window
    on the other side of the sun?
Will the fool in her fall on the swords protruding
    from the drapes of the covetous city's drawing room?
Will the pride of lions in her shoulders bear the weight
    of her own dark angel wounded in the rain?

It's in the cards. It's not in the cards
the heart of a mandolin hums in the hand
the jacks are holding oracle bones

in the pockets of their suits. It's in the cards
it's not in the cards. Past and sudden
revelations bring the house tumbling down
around the Queen of Clubs so pressed for time
It's in the cards. It's not in the cards
the present portends stasis and flush sails
picking up wind in the eyes of diamonds
looking out on the joker's wild eternity

There's a deck of cards face down on the table

Will the bridge spanning the abyss be there going and coming
    from the lady's armchair to the rim of the crowd?
Will she divine a way with more than string or ribbon
    to harness the dragon appearing in her field?
Will she learn to dance with her head brushing the clouds
    and her feet patterning figure eights in clover?

There's a deck of cards face down on the table

THE GREEN HARMONICA

The mouth begins a movement
along the orbits of celestial bodies
along the roof of the house of angels
along the line of least resistance
notes correspond with the heart's sudden ocean
conquering the walls
the breath inhales
a chord of joy and relief
unlocks the lid of longing
along the length of the green harmonica
green channels of distance flooded

The mouth begins a movement
a moment of hesitation
takes off with the speed of transient stars
and souls pursue their instinctive sail of the universe
green glasses shatter
green bar lights make the mirrors shine
green of the concrete floor
the breath exhales
trailed by a string of the brightest lanterns
breath that reaches the darkest corners of the room
breaks in the hollows between the reeds

Green wings beating against the ceiling
along the boulevards of the Milky Way
along the length of the green harmonica

OUT OF THE BLUE

The horses that carry me   have brought me
this far   as I reach for the sun   a skywriting plane
comes flying   out of the blue   a script of clouds
a wisp of hand   holding an old card of fortune
through a rip in the roof of the tent   oracles come flying

For my horses   flutes and drums have always
urged them over wastelands   they've carried my luggage
this far   full of prayer beads and photographs
they've carried me to all that's yet to be   bowed heads
in a circle of sawdust   heavy with blankets of roses
as I reach for the sun   their hearts are open   but
their yellow wings are slack with age   any moment
ancestral music   will call them away

As I watch them leave the spotlight   a fresh mount
is needed to lift me   above the circus   above
the tiers of somnambulists   the sermons of fire
and gnashing teeth   the dust blown in the eyes
of angels   on the midway   a million tours
of blind alleys   the bells that ring three times a day

reminding me to atone   above the safety nets
the halls of fright   and fleeing distractions
up to all that's yet to be

As I watch my horses leave the spotlight
a white steed comes   flying in the tail winds
of the skywriting plane   flying with the grace
and muscle of Al Borak   Black Beauty   Pegasus
Marengo   Rosinante   Trigger   Traveller
Silver   Native Dancer   Sea Biscuit   and Secretariat
a new horse comes
out of the blue
to lift me

up to the message in the script of clouds -

though escape by land and sea is blocked
still there's a way through the sky

up to the old card of fortune -

mount spirit wander at your ease

as I reach for the sun
through a rip in the roof of the tent
up to all that's yet to be

ST. GEORGE AND THE DRAGON

The night was an ocean. A river
a reservoir surrounded with empty bottles
teetering on the edge. The night
was swollen and gutted. A cold rain
fell on my hair and the bed sheets
exuded an odor of mildew and decay

Aqua grey drops of moisture
on the clammy walls

The night was inhabited
by a saurian daemon. It's foul
prehensile smell crawling
out of the basement. Part dog
part rat. Part winged
and scaly serpent. In the kitchen
it beat its long barbed tail
against a chair

The air swam through the motions
of being alive

You came into the ocean. The river
the reservoir. You came with your lance
bearing down on the throat
of the monster. Blood gushed
from its wound. It twisted. It groaned
and expired. And together
we found enough dry wood
to start a fire

LAND OF THE GREAT IMAGE

Popcorn. Venus in furs
That Touch of Mink
on the drive-in screen. The baby blue
eyes. A toothpaste smile
lighting up the sky
walls of anger. My walls of fire
flaring up into a solid red
movie screen
Oh, to be sexy and blond
like Doris Day
the most popular girl in town
and infinitely stupid

Blank screen. A can of coke
a ride through the night
in my dungarees
a ride through the night
with the radio on

He's a rebel,
and he'll never ever be any good.

He's a rebel,
cause he never never does what he should.

Chain smoking cigarettes
a ride through the night
on the highways stretching
over the Meadowlands
in New Jersey. The highways of sleep -
long corridors of Hypnos
lined with billboards
of the ultimate dream girl
drinking the ultimate
dream glass of milk
in the Land of the Great Image

FLYING NOWHERE

Head winds and rain
from New York to Shannon
but we're flying. Nowhere
don't bother packing
you won't need a toothbrush
we're flying. *Par Avion*

Watch the wide rover's wings
during takeoff
you don't have to fasten your seatbelt
if you're stuck on the aisle
and can't see the city
the dazzling lights
of Rockaway Boulevard
will always be there

We're flying. Nowhere

Over the ocean
lines from Yeats and O'Casey
are scrawled on the backs of the seats
even in Economy
the Chieftains are inside the headphones
and Van Morrison's latest CD
if you didn't bring valium
you're not going to need it

We're flying. Nowhere

Aer Lingus has duty-free shopping, in flight
Waterford crystal and Chanel No. 5
if you don't care for Jameson's
you can ask for a Guinness
if you don't like lasagne
there's chicken pot pie
if you don't like the movie
you don't have to watch it

We're flying. Nowhere

Nowhere. Nowhere
flying nowhere
nowhere. Nowhere. *Par Avion*

Pockets of turbulence may occur
the nose may take a dive
storms may darken the pilot's vision
and throw the plane off course
if you don't have a rosary
you can count on your fingers
if your life jacket's missing
you've still got a prayer

We're flying. Nowhere

Coming in for the landing
the plane glides like a sleigh
on a snow surface of clouds
to the right catch a glimpse
of the green coast of Ireland
keep calm and grip the arm rests
when the wheels hit the runway
and you'll be fine

We're flying. Nowhere

Going through customs
officials at Shannon
will want to see your passport
if the old one's expired
and you forgot to get a new one
or you left it behind in the kitchen
with the camera and the Baedeker's
don't worry

We're flying. Nowhere

Nowhere. Nowhere
flying nowhere
nowhere. Nowhere. *Par Avion*

Notebooks on the high street in Skibbereen
a sweater to bring home for Joe
the view of the stars from the crater
at Liss Ard
on your very last day
sitting sadly by the sea in Castletownshend
if you don't want to say goodbye
you won't have to

We're flying. Nowhere

Head winds and rain
from New York to Shannon
but we're flying. Nowhere
don't bother packing
you won't need a toothbrush
we're flying. *Par Avion*

Nowhere. Nowhere
flying nowhere
nowhere. Nowhere. *Par Avion*

THE PHILOSOPHER'S EGG

Into the desiccated night. The sun tied to the back of a lion
into the red combustible forest. Racing through trees
like a burnished planet. Passing behind clouds
a kingdom of hermits. An elusory lion
being sure not to step on the fires set off by his paws
in the tall dry grass birds burst in erotic display
a hot wind blows. The dead leaves that fall
are touched with the promise of preternatural ease

How exhilarating. A love chase
pursuing the prey over rivulets of mercury
tracking his scent to the steps of an old alchemist's
den where his bones lie down to slumber in stone
windows shatter from the heat. A piece of furniture. A roof beam
burns to feed the furnace. Roaring flacons
flasks and alembics cram the dusty shelves
a bubbling elixir. A metal-making alchemist
summoning me to approach in his greatcoat and mask
entreating me. To take the orb he offers in his hand

A golden egg
a ball of light
a vessel
of transformation
a gleaming matrix
opening to reveal
a tiny
hand-bound book
illustrated
with radiant lions

VOTIVE

As the dark velvet stage curtain falls
on the unsuspecting tail of the afternoon
lovers drop their victory wreaths
and enter the cathedral. To pray
for expensive operations
to sew them together forever

In the dim light of the votive candles
warm liquids run down between their legs

The purifying perfumes of frankincense
burn in the thurible. And roses
fill the air

Upon this consecrated ground. St. Michael
wrest the serpent from my heart. Unfix
the fangs.   And let the bird fly
into my vaulted ceilings of sky

Let the swirling clouds
of amorphic starlight
crystallize beside me
as my lover
warm and rested from his sleep

STAR PARTY

Following the curve of the Dipper's handle
warm summer torsos are high overhead
in the azure fields phantom fingers
pluck the strings of a harp
how can you keep your feet on the ground
with the Scorpion's heart the rival of Mars
it's a perfect night for a party

Moonless and clear the Milky Way
rises as smoke from a million candles
the head of Our Lady of Labyrinths
crowned with a wreath of asters
how can you shield your eyes from the mirror
with the Arrow striking a golden apple
it's a perfect night for a party

Get out your star maps and binoculars
we're going to stay out all night long
on the rooftops in Central Park
what good is heaven for
if you don't look at the sky

Thirty thousand light years from here
the history of an ancient race is written
on the dome of the Great Blue Mosque
a hero lies upside down in a burning shirt
how can you sleep through the overture of the universe
with crystal birds pursuing the Lion
it's a perfect night for a party

Get out your telescopes and naked eyes
we're going to stay out all night long
in the backyards in the camp grounds
what good is heaven for
what good is heaven for
what good is heaven for
if you don't look at the sky
look at the sky
look at the sky
look at the sky

SEVEN VEILS

Rain, rain sweeps through the streets
as they grow dim
the face of the moon is lost in the clouds
under the veil

A castle keep
the thousand tears of the forest
the window of an exiled queen
dark as the sun sunk under the earth
with her heart pierced through
she paces back and forth
breathing a thin air of hope

Rain, rain shrouds the buildings
in ghostly mist
ankle wings speed me along
under the veil

A horde of sparrows
the high green hedge of a garden
mazes of passages making it hard
for the songs to find their way
to the entrance from the center
music rises like a golden flood
over centuries of night

Rain, rain makes the heavens clear
relieving the sobs of despairing angels
from a high perch the eyes take measure
under the veil

A viper in hiding
bound with ropes and cords
desire's delirious spring
is locked within
longing to make it to the far world
beyond the aloofness of memory
molting in the frame of an antique mirror

Rain, rain the wind is strong
the branches bend low to their limit
light pours out of a buttonhole
under the veil

The blazing sails of a ship
the seaworthy masts of a caravel
heading out of the harbor
with an unfamiliar sextant
without a guide to the chaos of the sky
without a mission or goods to transport
sailing without reason to sail

Rain, rain heavier now
running in sheets off the rooftops
life's secret soul wells up
under the veil

The steadfast light of a hermit's lamp
fueling the emptiness
with impatient brightness
in the desert desolate and lonely
a flame held close to the chest
a season of victories waiting
in the shadow of hostile cliffs

Rain, rain here to stay
filling the holes from here to the river
a silent corridor lined with lions
under the veil

The evening dancer
emerging from a vermilion tent
with slippers of gold and a ruby choker
at the invitation of the infinite she dances
for him only will the wild dogs stay away
beyond the campsite in the pitch blackness
with the perils of cold sleep

Rain, rain makes a soft asylum
shielding me from a tireless hunter
nothing touches the nerve ends of the universe
under the veil

A map of the night in autumn
A jaded Pegasus in holding
marked by an absence of magnitude
still with one blow of his hoof
fountains spring forth
stable doors come down
and flight through a field of Arabian stars begins

ARIA

With bewitching sweetness
the deep song of sleep
lures you away
behind her veiling Spanish shawl

I'm left with your soul's breath
the smell of sex
and the meteorites at the window
casting a shower of diamonds
over our skin

Unconquerable isometric crystals
older than the earth's mantle
older than the moon's crust
dispersing prismatic colors
forged in the fires of the first casting mold

Victorious dark-eyed sleep
embraces you with embroidered flowers
and the deep song
of subterranean waterfalls

I run my hand across your chest

It comes away with diamond dust
destined to be scattered
wide among the stars when we die
returning to our source in the sky

FRIENDSHIP WITH THE VIRGIN

Mother of air. We walk so closely
together. With the cool autumnal
sand between our toes. A lavender
sea. Breezes blowing through
the white Egyptian layers of your robes
so soft and scented. Powdered
and pink. Your skin is your sachet
stripped and bare. The lonely
sky mourns the loss of its blueness

Bluer and deeper than hyacinth blue
or mazarine blue. Stronger
than cyanine blue. A dark blue
stronger than Flemish blue
hummingbirds. Your eyes in contrast
to the sky's are sapphire wings

Where pale grey cliffs
slope down
into the sea. I'm born
with your arms around me

MY MACUMBA

A bird crashed out of the sky
his spirit lodged in my throat
I could feel it choking me
and I couldn't breathe

Macumbeira spread out her shells on the table

"My daughter," she told me
"The hand of your Mother, Iemanja, will hold you
The Queen of the sea is your saint
You'll fall down. But when the spirit leaves you
it will be as though he never existed
Go and bathe in the essence
of white medicinal roses
then make your appeal to the saint."

Waves broke into stallions
mottled grey in the night
I lit a candle
and walked to the edge of the ocean
pouring wine for the goddess

A bird cried out in my throat to be free

I fell down
and when his spirit left me
my innocence
my self-confidence
returned

THE MAN WITH THE SCARLET KNEE BANDS

Heart be still
be quiet

Though impressions
burn in you
like fires
out of control

Be still
be quiet

Throw buckets
on the hot stones
you set out so feverishly
to walk upon

Be calm
be confident in your goal

The man with the scarlet knee bands
will come

The man will come
to breathe on your hands
and bathe your feet
with water
from an invisible world

Be still

Be full of hope
and expectations
and mindful
of the mystery of things

For he will come
down a long, long
stairwell of approach

He will come
the man with the scarlet knee bands
will come

To join you
and hold you
in a yellow light
that fills your holes

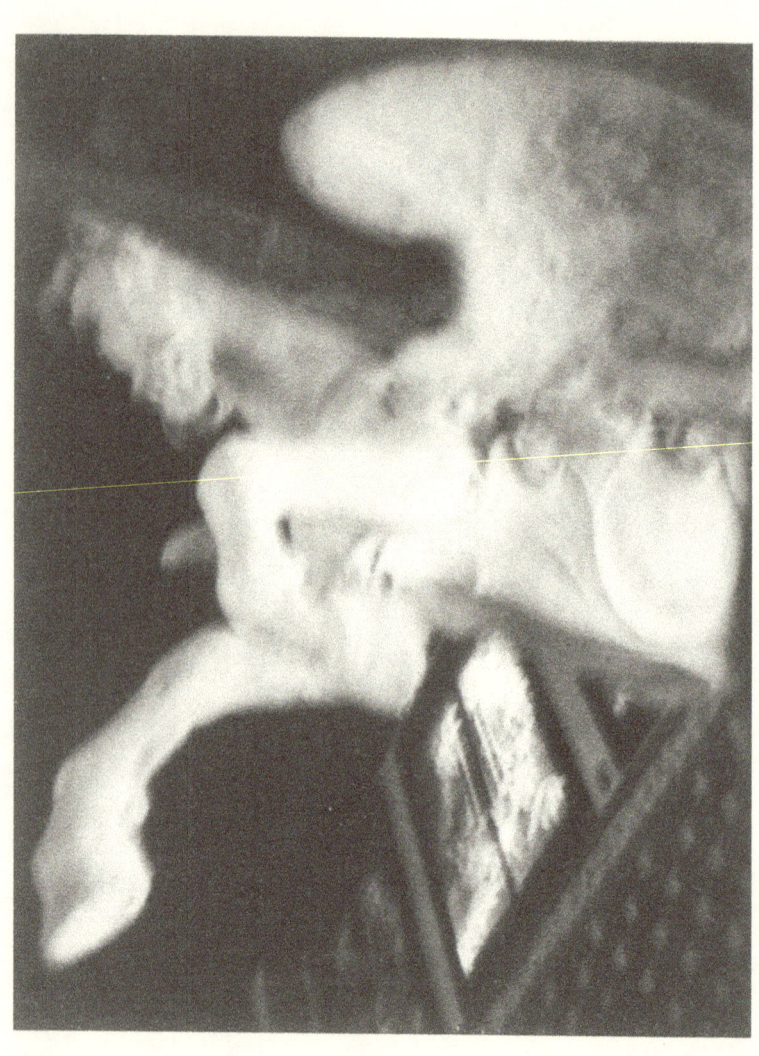

SOVEREIGNTY OF THE CLOUDS

Up from idle gazings. Ubiquitous vertigo
catapults me into the sky's consensual arms. Up
from the supine meadow. A life line gathers me
to the threshold of summer's restful reign

In dry light. Horses levitate towards the sun
bending long white necks beneath a burden
of coronets and interwoven fruit. O seasonal arousal
of angels. Impulsive air gathers me in a train
of fleecy lace moving windward

Treasure galleons. Sails of silk. Blooms
of foxglove. Phlox. Oriental poppy
plumes of ostrich. Albino tigers. Turreted tents
blithe hierarchies of canyons. Converging

Around an altar of alabaster. Fire fingers
spread to the extent of their domain. Lifting
a chalice to my lips. To drink
of time's endurance

OPEN WINDOW

The air is cool. Coming
with the tourmaline sea
into my symphonic interior
caresses. Both yours
and the breeze's lingering
longer days of dazzling
light flood the room
above the Avenue of Palms

A bed with the imprint
of your body on it. Sugar
almonds on a silver tray
posing as if for a painting
before a Moorish screen
four goldfish swim in a bowl
on fire. My skin is blushing
pink like a battle of roses

After a bath. The charged
idleness accompanying
your absence wraps around me
in the silk of a white kimono
in the frame of the open
window. I can see my buoyant
heart. Sailing the Mediterranean
with a wind caught
under its wings

MOVING STAR

Lightning striking   fluorescent serpents

This wave of hot chrome metal breath over my spine

Let's have another drink

while the hailstones and demon rain
bounce off the corrugated roadhouse roof

Let's swallow our spirits
and obliterate the night

*

> *Moving star*
> *bird of fire*
> *open your wings across the sky*

A white hot poker
this fervent tongue
is burning a hole in my spine

> *O ceaseless opal phoenix, sing!*

Let's have another drink

while the thunder roars
and spreads its dread
a hundred miles around

Let's put another quarter in the jukebox

    *

   Moving star
   bird of fire
   your light is a voice

Oblivion

   your light is a song

utter oblivion

   blowing the veils
   away from my eyes

obliterated in a long black tunnel of clouds
we drove the car   weird insect harmonies
currents of air   violent, vertical movements
of heat escaping the ground surface
the shock to the eyes   bloody green toads
and dismembered lizards falling out of the sky
an army of locusts alighting on the windshield
we drove the car on   into the dark Dakota night
longing   longing for unnamable things

    *

Lightning striking   fluorescent serpents

These sudden waves of gasoline breath over the spine

Let's have another drink

while the thunder roars

Let's have another drink

full of smoke   noise   and confusion

SPELLBOUND

Spellbound. Words escape me. Going out
as if a flame. Extinguished. My capacity
to want anything

In this transport the temperature is dropping
on the top floor of the walk up. The mane
of a nameless horse. Tossed back
among the waves in your eyes. The blue heaven
and the open sea bringing the sundered night
to an end. In the web of separate things
the flight of the night's lost bird is ending
on the most remote corner of the world
an explosion in me. Lying in the ashes
of a dress. My ember wings make a last fluttering gasp
knowing they've seen enough. Downstairs
the linoleum is covered with a carpet
of bleeding prayers and the walls and ceiling
take on its glow. No other hand but yours
reaches out of the sky-drifts
to check the fire. No other hand

Spellbound. Words escape me. Going out
as if a flame. Extinguished. My capacity
to want anything

In this transport the temperature is dropping
in a cold ray of moonlight
on your bed
I pass away
annihilated
from head to foot
in the fortress
of your aloneness

BOY BLUE

Weary of waiting, blue boy. Following the map
of a vanished sea. Blue lights in the harbor
blue sails carry you through twilights
obscuring your lodestar with dusk. Dark-adapted eyes
in the period of blindness, between the gods departed
and the gods yet to come, all that is rare and excellent
furnish your happy isle's watchtower of white
all that you seek. All the soul's companions
the music of grazing horses plays on the shore

Shaped by the charity of the firmament, blue boy
gold scales begin to rise. Over the water, at the edge
of the dreamline, prevailing winds favor a crossing
go on ahead. The deepest chamber of the night
will restore your exhausted wings. Go on ahead
there, there is pleasing variety in the moon and stars
awaiting your imprint. The shimmer of leaves
breathes a song without words
and corals lie lost from the track of the world

A THOUSAND YEARS

How goes the night?
how goes the watch?
as midnight approaches
in the storm waves of the sky
the moon beats a gnarled fist
on her old yellow drum
a thousand years
have passed away
a thousand years
are yet to come

How goes the night?
how goes the watch?
a lone sailboat makes its way
through tolling towers
sounded by the motion of the sea
a thousand years
fill the hold with dust and desire
a thousand years
of wasted wings to set free

Fragile the wilderness
the skeleton bells ring
for eternal return
another March breeze
blowing across the planet
another life with new idols
and the same concerns

How goes the night?
how goes the watch?
flood waters swallow enfeebled horses
fallen from the cracks in the dome
a thousand years of races
in the funeral beds
a thousand years of fits and starts
before we're home

How goes the night?
how goes the watch?
in the end there's a full single sail
propelled by its own will
a thousand years
bring a pale beacon
with the coming dawn
a thousand years
of moving forward and standing still

Fragile the wilderness
the skeleton bells ring
for eternal return
another March breeze
blowing across the planet
another life with new idols
and the same concerns

SLEEPING GYPSY

The tongue is unsatisfied   firebird sweets
a morsel   a taste of carrion   sleep
desire will have its form
and beasts go forth   as in a dream
your belly warm as birth
the newborn skulls of coyotes ripping through
like eggteeth in a dance of bones
of spinning light
the frantic tongue
insatiable

Sleeping gypsy scatter your horns
the animal parts
the dangling limbs of tapestries
prey of the huntsman   St. Julian
his relentless bow and divinity for madness
his angel ecstasy for animals
blood pudding   firebird sweets

It's not the time for siestas of lions
sleeping gypsy
desire will be your beast
and its jaws roll around a moan
of ageless stones
primeval
prankster
fork your tongue
like a dragon
spit

INSOMNIE

The black tie skating rink
the silver blades etching a codex
hypnos of mirrors
the reflective surface
of polished obsidian
scratches

The revolving hypnotic disc

Thirty-three revolutions
playing diversions
over
and over
elegant ladies
cutting figure eights
on the vinyl table
embraced by a silver arm
with its needle
caught in a groove
of perpetual imaginings

TOMB FOR OPHELIA

Gently, lifeless. After his play. Her toy in blood
no longer harms the river nesting in orisons
Though day it is. The wild white roses of her face
and palms collect the bright stagnation of anointed moons
more tears in floods. More sighing and lamenting
did she see his antic disposition. Did her heart
beat down between her legs. Did he lie there

Gently, lifeless. The pendant boughs of willow
couldn't bear the weight of her. Holding columbines
and cornflowers. Rosemary and rue. Grieving
without judgment. Divided from herself. The greying
grace of her gown buoying a sacrificial bride
the black clouds of his mourning suit in the center
of her eyes. Fixed on a heaven too high to climb

FAN MOTIF AT NOH-THEATRE

Cranes and pine trees
painted on a gold-leafed fan
the gentle
the wind, wood

The image of the cliff
overlooking the ocean

A safe place to be
for the lovers
finding a resting place
on their long flight
from the water to the sky

The male is seated
on a branch of the pine trees
drawing his lover near to the nest
his lover
who wrestles with the winds
that impair her landing

REQUIEM

New York City, September 11, 2001

The precious skyline of glass and steel remains
Of all that's lost
And flowing into the sea
At the end of the island where the rivers meet

The candles burn for so many
Doves crowd the branches
Of the blue garden tonight

In every park on every corner a fine curtain of dust
Settles on the altars
Of the open city
Photographs and the sweet heavy fragrance of flowers

The candles burn for so many
Doves crowd the branches
Of the blue garden tonight

So many wings rising from so many lives ended
In the collapse of the towers
A common prayer
Scribbled on scraps of paper blows through the streets

The candles burn for so many
Doves crowd the branches
Of the blue garden tonight

Beneath the bridges the rivers flow as sorrow into the sea
Of all that's passing
Innocence and ashes
The precious skyline of glass and steel remains

SEA FEVER

Under the bridge the water is full of ships
if it could quake my heart would wrest away from
its guards and assume a throne as tall
as a topmast moving out to sea. Beneath
a crown of stars hymnal sails in the ascendant
night's moist consummate air carrying me to
a wilderness beach where the rest of me waits
beside your side

A tide of horses swims through the swollen black
lanes to the moon. A weight of wanting
roped to their backs

At a dead gallop. The waves would break me
if I could open in your wide white arms
a prodigal mermaid with eyes on fire. Buoyed
by love's wild wings. Eastward leaning
in the phosphorous sky where the ocean gathers
high towards heaven. My summer skin
of silk and mother-of-pearl drinks
in the still asylum of a blue sound

PHANTOM VESSEL

The exiled skins of lemons. Sucked
and strewn over the floor. The tongue
parched and swollen. Bleached by heat
its thoughts smoldering cinders
consumed in a razed garden. Beyond
the room the trees twist in the wind. Anarchic
constellations of the summer night
swirl in the sky. Haphazard myths
above the water line

The reflection of a restless alignment -

A night full of mares
kicking up dust
on its immanent desert island

To set foot outside the room
To set foot upon the shore

To walk towards a phantom vessel -
an elusive clipper
setting foot on the seas
void of destination
or port of call

Sailing
to be engulfed
in the tempest
of Serpens
Tucana
and Triangulum

DARK SKIES

How far they are from paradise. In the grass
at the end of the parking lot. A handful of magi
rowing a boat through a neglected passage
of longitude. Dressed like mendicants. Fallen
from an elevated oasis. Without turbans of gold
or embroidered coats. Only faded linen
replicas of leopard skins

Behind them the eastern night. The guard dogs
at the burial grounds barking into the empty tombs
where the stars of summer were interred. In rows
of glass coffins. Stars from the pale blue wings
of a swan. Stars to move the rocks and trees
with songs. The dolphin's stars

Now missing from the fresco over the city
the lion's silver goblets overturned. Where last
the supper sat. A crystal cob-webbed chandelier
hangs in an infirmary of pigments. No wind
no current stirs the still life. Just bowls of dust
flooded with light. The scraps uneaten

Spots of a thousand eyes
dropping like flies
dropping like flies

DOOR TO DOOR

Now I lay me down   weary of reading
indecipherable maps   relieved of the weight of amulets
and timepieces   I lay me down   on cool white sheets
on a pillow with a key of gold   I lay me down to open
the doors where all that is stalled lifts off in dreams

A door opens on Lorca   standing with his back
to the camera in a courtyard in Spain   wings protruding
from the shoulders of his white linen suit   on the front lawn
of my childhood home a door opens on maple trees
filled with light   I sing to them and angels appear
in the upper branches   in the deserts of Venus
a door opens on a pale horse turning pink in the rosy glow
of the setting sun   all that is stalled lifts off in dreams
birds of ruby glass alight on the pilings of a pier
over the Hudson   a door opens on the palms
of my hands scarred with hearts and wands   crosses
glyphs and planets   assuring my good fortune
to get lost in a movie palace   circling a sarcophagus
filled with sand from the Valley of the Kings
deep in outer space   a door opens on Neil Young
the sky pilot flying from point to point to fire the stars
with a gas torch igniter   and all that is stalled
lifts off in dreams

On a bed rimmed with flowers and the yellow pollen
that glistens on my skin in the dark   I lay me down
on cool white sheets   on a pillow with a key of gold
I lay me down to open the doors where all that is stalled
lifts off in dreams

A door opens on a courtyard   deep in outer space
in the palms of my hands   the night opens at last

ALTAR PIECE

No guide   but a faceless compass   this night
gathered in the tent cloth of the last encampment
I send up my sighs   beyond the perimeter   to the point
from where I fell   I send up my sighs   the equal
of astral winds   blowing over the poles of a ship

This night   for a germ of light to take hold
the altar is dressed with the soft and hard sounds
of the letters   a wrought iron bell from the gate
of the winged white horse   rosemary
in remembrance of what has been spoiled
and feathers for flight

Where the dark sea breaks into the dark night
I send up my sighs

*

In what repository of time   trapped   in what
latitude   lost in the halls of a vandalized labyrinth
in what Tropic   of Hazard or Rigid Inertia

over whose bowl of worms
do I stand   repeating   repeating
to what end do I declare myself   to what end

Seal of Wisdom
Vault of Change
Mystical Lantern
Cabinet of Solitude

Open to me   open to me

*

As it was in the beginning   I saw the gauze
withdrawing from the blueprints of the liminal library
the doors of the stable flew apart   to the hit of stars
proclaiming holes in the ceremonial sky   in the east
the canopy of the ecstatic forest was excavated   hands
unraveled every sail   at the water's edge   a platinum
flute   inexhaustible by a single note in any language
took me to moist clay tablets
holding their breath

In all directions
hoof beats
sounded

in and out
of sleep
white   black
yellow   red
through a gauntlet
of mercurial wands

          *

Now   all is quiet   only my sighs   gathered
in the tent cloth of the last encampment   the far away
stampede within this night   a photo of young Venus
with an arrow and bow   above   my constellation
is in free fall   where it comes down   a boatman
awaits the signal   to row the frayed pages
of a book of prayer to the center of rest

So that a germ of light might take hold
so that the winged white horse
might be freed from the rock
so that I might ring the bell
and walk in concert
with syllables
out of my head
so that a thousand birds
might intercede
so that I might know
to what end
do I declare myself
to what end

I offer these words

SACRIFICE End

Gone away   gone away
across the wide white sea
you can close your eyes

All the pain is gone

The moonless shores
are towering and steep
frozen reliquaries of sleep

Forever is the mercy
of the polar night

No flaming nimbuses
no hell
no crown of petrified thorns
no hope trembling
no knives ripping
through the silk on your back
no wings of Baal's angels
casting shadows

before you and behind
no wind
no sacrament of rain
nothing remains

You can bid your boat away

All the pain is gone

In a rapture of bones
flesh   fluids   veins
and dreams
of long lines of leopards
in the snow

HOMAGES

I, FELLINI

8½
in the sky
over the scaffolding
for the space ship launch

My happiness
is this bullhorn
and straw fedora
in the blistering sun
of Cinecitta

On the birthday
of Studio 5's youngest grip
my friends
you've toasted me
and my new film
with spumante in paper cups
and in return
I'd like to say

Grazie amici!

I, Fellini
in my forty-third year
of beautiful confusion
have been hired
to shoot a masterpiece
and I will
riddle the Sistine ceiling
with buckshot

Kidding, only kidding

I, Fellini
will shoot Mastroianni
in a perfectly cut Milanese suit

Mastroianni
with greying hair
and sad dark circles
under his eyes -
the Adonis of despair -
I will shoot Mastroianni
in such a light
women the world over
will want him
in their Roman beds
Chinese beds
beds in the U.S.A.
even outer space

I, Fellini
who am nothing
without my crew
the actors and actresses
all the extras
the extravagant
black and white palette
of Gherardi
di Venanzo's magic lens
and primo maestro
Nino Rota's score -
to let you know
the circus
of the spheres

I, Fellini
who am nothing
if not my own creation

will shoot Mastroianni
into the stratosphere
in film number eight
and a half

Si, otto e mezzo

Primo, The White Sheik
then *I, Vitelloni*
La Strada
Il Bidone
Le Notti di Cabiria
La Dolce Vita
and *The Temptations of Dr. Antonio* -
as you know
a complete film
within *Boccaccio '70*
Variety Lights I don't count
I shared the director's credit
with Lattuada

Le mezzo?

Agenzia matrimoniale
from *Amore in Citta*, 1953
only thirty-two minutes

I, Fellini
who am nothing
without you
have been hired
to shoot a masterpiece
and I will
lift it off the storyboards
from the comic strip
in my mind -
Mandrake
and Mastroianni
up into the stratosphere

Soon, today, now

We can start whenever you like
just say the magic words -
asa nisi masa -
and we'll all be rich
to each and every one
an Alfa Romeo
four cases of spumante
and an apartment
on the Via Veneto

Your part, Marcello?
you ask about your part

I see you like me
in a state of beautiful confusion
following a nuclear disaster
a director, terrified
of making his next film
boarding a space ship -
the new Noah's ark -
with friends and associates
you'll fly to Mars
and marry a nice Martian girl -
una bella ragazza
with fishy scales
and a single eye in her forehead

Well, maybe not
maybe three eyes
in her forehead
who knows?
I'm still working
on the concept

I see you making love
to your Martian bride
but it won't be enough
it's never enough

we always want more
don't we *amico*?

You'll have a harem
of exotic space girls -
Anouk, Sandra,
my lovely Saraghina -
on Christmas Eve
in the Martian snow
you'll walk through the door
with presents under your arms
for all of them
they'll bathe you
and caress you
but it won't be enough
it's never enough

You'll sit by a fountain
listening to your inner voice
just like me
you'll hear nothing
niente, niente, niente

I've said enough
let's begin
before we destroy
this film
with talk

At the end, we'll begin at the end

Maurice, my ringleader
have you got your top hat?

Eccellente!

Now hoist me up on the dolly
let's have the clowns

with their instruments -
tuba, clarinet, French horn -
and the little boy
with his flute
in his white cape and cap

I want them in the middle

All the actors and actresses
all in white
position yourselves
along the rim of the circus ring
everyone hold hands
and spread out together

Maurice, when I give you the sign
you're to look
straight into the camera
and say -
"Life is a great white movie screen
Let's step into it together!"

Marcello, when you hear
those words
you'll step up on the rim
and join the parade

Are we ready?

Asa nisi masa

All quiet on the set

Azione!

RED HILLS AND SKY
(after Georgia O'Keeffe)

In the sky I am walking
a black bird
flying over Ghost Ranch
loud and raw
under my feet
the red hills still
touch my heart
as they never touched
anyone else's

I saw something
I wanted to say

In the miles
and miles
of badlands
all the earth colors
of the painter's palette
were out there -
the light Naples' yellow
to the ochres
orange, red
and purple earth -
even the soft
earth green

I saw something
I wanted to say

Driving past
on a trip
to the Navajo country
clean white bones
and bare red hills
rolled away
beyond the windows
of the Model A Ford -
the easiest car
I ever had
to work in -
in the lonely
feeling place
called Ghost Ranch

I saw something
I wanted to say

I unbolted
the driver's seat
turned it around
and painted
with a 30 x 40 canvas
on the back seats
until four
in the afternoon
when the bees
were going home

I painted
a black bird
flying between the arms
of two red hills
reaching out
to the brilliant sky
and holding it

HEATHROW SUNFLOWER
for Benn Northover

The distant latitude of festival tents   a motor car on
country lanes   the medal around your colt's neck
in the breakfast room of the Swan Hotel   a saint
brought back from Spain   looking out
at Southwold's cobbled streets   the salty air
the pages of the registry   as far as anyone
could remember   you were an unexpected angel
waving to Hamlet from the pebbled beach
Hamlet waving back from Elsinore

Presently   Heathrow's a green meridian running
to the base of the sunflower you hold   my heart safe
from black marauders exterminating the attic room
an ocean away   on the Underground   we have
a long ride to Wood Green   my eyes are dead
your eyes are red   running film all night   on the streets
of Paris   *Howl* and *Zone* on your cell phone
in the rain   Covet Garden's a cave of a café
where you sheltered me   in candlelight

Tomorrow   will be a mound of Christmas trees
discarded in a vacant lot   in Brooklyn
the pewter coin you fondle will slip through your fingers
falling   face up on a bar room floor
the feather pen of the saint from Spain will guide me
on your birthday   with your brother and the one
with stars in her pockets   I'll wish you well
before more than hazard determines the interception
of our paths   we'll speak at length
of the pilgrim's way   and friendship

THE ENIGMA OF BUSTER KEATON

1.

I looked out the window of the train into the pink-golden
sands of the desert. Into the blank incandescent infinity
looking at a sunset on Venus. The book on my lap
was open to THE ENIGMA OF BUSTER KEATON
the small white Egyptian in a linen suit. Walking
through the snow with a straw boater and cane

Palm trees. Swimming pools. The back lots of the studios
the endless possibilities of silence

I looked out the window
into the eyes of the mystery
on a platform
outside the high Spanish ceilings
of Union Station

2.

A crowd of photographers and reporters surrounded him
in his snow shoes. A school of parasites on the gills
of an angel fish. Light bulbs flashed. The exposure
caused discomfort. He was moving fast. But
not fast enough to elude them

"Excuse me, sir, but can you explain
your divine comic invention
improvisation
and spontaneity?"

"Why don't you use a script?"

"How do you come up with all the gadgets?"

"Can you explain your lucidity?"

He turned with his usual grace. It was vaguely
reminiscent. He tried to place his feet on the ground
the gravity wasn't there

"Excuse me, sirs. I beg you to leave me alone
I've awoken from sleep into a nightmare
too vast and unimaginative. Please, my eyes
are painful. The high Spanish ceilings are calm
but I can't see the cherubs gathering about the rafters
I'm suspended in vertigo. My car is waiting
please, I can't keep it waiting

To answer your questions before I go

I use the silence precisely
naturally and intuitively."

3.

I took a cab to the tall iron gates and proceeded
up the driveway leading to the villa. Weeds
came up through the stones under my feet
vines grew over the toy house for the children
in the moonlight the vegetation was lush and alive
invigorated by a Santa Ana wind

I knocked on the door. It opened on a young blond
taking her silver fox into the manicured night

"He's waiting for you in his bedroom," she said
then ran across the lawn

Potted palms. Persian rugs. The endless procession
of extras dancing to a jazz band

4.

A maid took my wrap. I was directed to a table
with champagne and hors d'ouevres.   It was hard to guess
the number of people under the chandeliers
the ballroom was filled to capacity

I sipped my drink and observed the flames going off
before me. Floor-length gowns sequined with rubies
diamonds. Falling into the arms of perfumed volcanoes

The bandleader called for an intermission

I made my way up the wide congested stairwell

There were rooms leading off the landing like voyages
in one men played pool
in another women talked of jewels and fame

5.

A stream of candle light swam out from a crack beneath the door
at the end of the hallway. I walked over and knocked
it opened slightly. Inside I could see THE ENIGMA
OF BUSTER KEATON in a linen suit playing with a set
of trains on the floor. The snow fell all around. A thin
layer settled on the tops of the furniture throughout

I stood there wondering about his ability to travel
he sensed my presence behind him and turned around
sending a sliver of dry ice into my bloodstream
with his wide pharaohnic gaze

The train set was located in the middle of the room
they were band-new. French passenger trains
driving through snow storms in the Alps
with a strong light on the silver engine to guide the way
beside a royal blue butterfly umbrella lying on the floor

He picked it up and walked towards the open windows
a wind caught under the flaps of his pockets
and lifted him off the floor into a series of somersaults

"Where do you go when you're not dreaming?
when you're not in love
when the oppressive contagion of reality engulfs you?"

He took my hand and led me through the movements

BLUE TANGO SHOES
for Patti on her 60th birthday

From New York to London and back again
the courses of our cryptic mythologies
soar in mid flight, converge, and go their separate ways
in a bookstore window in Buenos Aires
you saw sparkling blue tango shoes
and thought of the mariner off shore in the distance
adrift from the gold and silver canvas of your world
that fits so perfectly - a shirt of star field cloth

Always there's a porcelain angel
in the pitch and roll of my study
the blue tango shoes take their place
among the saints and rosaries
brought back from your Pythagorean travels
notebooks like this new one from the Argentine
a box of twenty-five eggs of semi-precious stone
and the last armless soldier from a box of one hundred
we bought on Second Avenue

Miniature blue tango shoes
blue roses and feathers on the toes, blue ankle straps
from Borges' city, which you didn't care for much
"Too much like a Portuguese city," you said
yet prowled the streets nonetheless
looking for treasures to stock the hold of my heart
and in return this poem -
a vial of pale green seawater
to wear around your neck

K E R O U A C

I had nothing   but I had a grey tee shirt
and I ironed on black velvet letters

K E R O U A C

I had nothing   I had four walls on St. Marks Place
a bottle of Calvados   and the silence of the universe
I had nothing   but I had you

From sea to shining sea   east to west   north to south
Atlantic   Pacific   Arctic   Antarctic   the Indian Ocean
and the eighth mar incognito   over   under   inside
and out   beyond everything   I had you   I had words
lines   and paragraphs rushing down mountainsides
high above the timber line   from Desolation Peak
to 242 choruses of blues for the Buddha and fellaheen
of Mexico City and every other place   I had your
footprints on the beach in Tangiers   your palm print
on the wheel of impermanence   your dreams of long
childhood walks under the old trees of New England
your athlete's body   your flannel shirts
your handsome face on a fire escape on E. 7th Street
just before the invocation of Duluoz   inhaling
one last Lucky Strike for the pent-up   aching

restless road   farewell subterraneans and water towers
of Manhattan   it was time for all that coming back
to America   the Lincoln Tunnel   oil tanks
and anemic skies in New Jersey   Route 80
over the Delaware   the road unraveling   the road
sufficient unto itself   a twentieth century
pilgrim's way   a home for the tathagata passing
through the railroad earth   the gas station night
the bebop radio wail of Charlie Parker's saxophone
clear across Kansas   to San Francisco   the little alley
off Market Street   Tokay in a paper bag
at the mouth of Bixby Canyon   Big Sur's ocean roar
of vowel sounds   from the far side of eternity
the waves laying better than a thousand transcendental
diamonds of compassion at your feet   even to the end
I had you   to the maenads of fame   tearing
you to pieces   in the glow of the television set
in Florida   to what's buried in Lowell's Edson Cemetery
Ti Jean   nothing's buried there   the dust
of your sacred bleeding catholic heart   with that
of the holy ghost   and certain mad and driven
saints   has been placed among the stars

I had nothing   but I had a grey tee shirt   and I ironed
on black velvet letters

K   E   R   O   U   A   C

DOOM'S DAY PIE
for Zara Kane

The red has to go. It's beyond darkness
the seascapes dropped dead a long time ago
the quiet dim of Muswell Hill will be all right for two
we have our books and a doom's day pie
we have poached cod, pie crust and sautéed leeks
enough to feed the multitude

In the event of a mothership landing in Regent Park
in the event of aliens occupying both Houses of Parliament
in the event of panic at Euston Station
there's a slice for you, a slice for me
and whoever remains amidst the debris

Delicious! With a demi-bouteille of Chablis
left over from my flight from New York
to the health of our unwritten pages!
may they flow one into another into a holy heap
a mountain of mesmerizing chapters
fit to endure the day of doom

When the Loch Ness monster floats down the Thames
in an inner tube. Pterodactyls take up the trees
on Victoria Road. The red bleeds off the walls
of its own and the seascapes flood the halls and more

We shall survive
for the pie will provide

BYRON'S TIME SHEET

Good Lord! Byron's set sail. Never to return
one lame foot planted firmly on the deck
never to return. A dismal shroud
draped on Dover's cliffs. Dalliance with him
is involuntary sport. But he doesn't get paid
for loving his sister, the likeness of himself
not with fame springing overnight and Caroline Lamb's
scene at Lady Heathcote's ball. He doesn't get paid
for that. Not with Dr. Polidori and a staff
of retainers fleeing the snub of Mayfair's beau monde
He doesn't get paid for that. No

He gets paid for clerking in a bookstore. That's
what he gets paid for. At twenty-eight he's going grey
but he doesn't get paid for that. He's clocked
fourteen hours on his time sheet for one entire year!
But he'll never get paid for it. No. He'll never get paid!

Good Lord! Byron's thrown himself on a chambermaid
in Brussels. But he doesn't get paid for that
what he earned from *Childe Harold*, Cantos I & II
was spent in a fortnight. Never to return
friendships with him are always passions
but he doesn't get paid for sharing a boat
with Percy Bysshe in the turbulent waves
on Lake Geneva. No. He doesn't get paid
for being fortified with brandy and laudanum
and stepping into the dungeon at the Castle of Chillon
no. He doesn't get paid for that

Good Lord! Byron's appetites have pursued him
over the Alps. Never to return. His travelling coach
is equipped with a wash tub. But he doesn't get paid
for that. Not with Burke's sublime in the sheer drop
before him and avalanches every five minutes
he doesn't get paid for that. He doesn't get paid
for two years in Venice in the Palazzo Moncenigo
on the Grand Canal. No. Not when he's standing
on the Bridge of Sighs with the Occident in one hand
and a turban in the other. He doesn't get paid for that

He gets paid for clerking in a bookstore. That's
what he gets paid for. At thirty-two he's going grey
but he doesn't get paid for that. He's clocked
fourteen hours on his time sheet for one entire year!
But he'll never get paid for it. No. He'll never get paid!

Good Lord! Byron's set to work on *Don Juan*
"a little finely facetious upon everything." But
he won't get paid for it. Not if he's taken as his mistress
the wife of an Italian count. No. Not if he's storing guns
for the Carabinieri. He doesn't get paid for that
He doesn't get paid for yachting with the English colony
at Pisa or witnessing the burning of Shelley's body
on the beach. No. He doesn't get paid for swimming
out to his schooner, the *Bolivar*, to exorcise
his violent remorse. No. He doesn't get paid for that

Good Lord! Byron's landed in Missolonghi. Never
to return. One lame foot planted firmly on the ground
Never to return. He's been named by unanimous vote
to the Greek Committee. But he doesn't get paid
for that. He doesn't get paid for advancing loans
to the patriots and parading in native dress. No
he doesn't get paid for riding out in the rain

and returning drenched in an open boat. He doesn't
get paid for throwing himself at destiny and leaving
his heart behind. No. He doesn't get paid for that

He gets paid for clerking in a bookstore. That's
what he gets paid for. At thirty-six he's going grey
but he doesn't get paid for that. He's clocked
fourteen hours on his time sheet for one entire year!
but he'll never get paid for it. No. He'll never get paid!

MOON MUSIC

1.

In a courtyard on the moon
the dust blows
over the bottom of the sea
to silence her broken cords
the dust blows

At the bottom of the sea
the milky neck and torso
of a lost guitar
over the frets and hollow
the dust blows

*Luna maria, luna maria
luna maria, luna maria*

In a courtyard on the moon
waiting for the one
to hold her
the guitar cries
from the bottom of the sea

The guitar cries for fingers
long and tapering
to make her music
in a courtyard on the moon
the guitar cries

*Luna maria, luna maria
luna maria, luna maria*

2.

Draped as the sonata
of summer's end
the emptiness of the moon
spills from under the lid
of a grand piano
taking up the sky

A wave as warm
as the sex of the moon
carries her through corridors
of sea hands
assaulting her negligee's
blossoming florescence
that dies away

In a spent beaching
of teeth, foam, seaweed tresses
and white mammal nakedness
the moon looks up
at what fashioned her at first -
an extended movement
of tonic and dominant keys

3.

I've come out early tonight
on my balcony
lowering myself over the line
of your horizon
I can't hear your music
filling the tide pools

I've come out early tonight
in a blue gown
all the silver and feldspar
you gave me
and the earrings
of rare white coral

Like my path now
on your broken surface
I tossed and turned all day
unable to sleep
I was agitated
behind my balcony

"The seas will be full again,"
my seahorse said
"Tranquility will be full again,
you'll see. The earth will wet
your thighs with his waves"

I've come out early tonight
with pearls in my hair
searching the beaches
extending a moon bow
showing my hand free of the ring
of the red planet

"Once more the oysters will rise
They'll face the earth,
open their shells and be fertilized
by earth dew"

I've come out early tonight
on my balcony
to tell you -
look at the sky behind you
look at the blood of Mars
mixed with my tears

4.

In the sky
that's never seen
she reclines
on a flowered divan
it's night
eternal night
but her eyes
are accustomed
to it

She has a table-top
reflecting scope
the gift of Newton
himself
in the sky
that's never seen
she luxuriates
in calculations
made
from observations

Stacks
of computations
the fruits of her
deliberations
are piled high
on her patio
there's no wind
to mess her hair
no clouds
to obstruct
her view
no rain
to bounce off
her umbrella

A star beams down
a spotlight
and she notes
in careful script:
how far
are the moons
of Jupiter?
at what speed
will Mercury's rotations
begin to hum?
how long
will it take
for the doors
of time
to open,
however slightly?

Half her life
she spends
in the sky
that's never seen
accompanied
by crustaceans
the musicians
in her court
who play
what they remember
of a suite
for ancient seas

5.

Over the estuaries
with his back to the sea
he left her. When her nets
no longer brought treasures
to the surface. He left her
in a pale green
paper-thin dress. For the open
knees of a newer moon
he left her. A hungry death

"Old hag, old hag,"
the children cry
it's time to move,
time to move along"

Up from the beaches
they hurl the wreckage
to accelerate her going
they throw stones
and shards. Shells
splinters of driftwood
and glass
cut her feet

"It's time to move along"

She gathers dignity
beads from a broken string
petals of hemlock
from his last bouquet
a rabbit fur is all she has

to warm her. In the cold
of her transit the highway
describing her orbit
ends on a plain
picked clean by gulls

"Time to move, old hag"

In the throws of her pale green
paper-thin dress. She closes
her eyes. Her hands
muffling a canticle

6.

A keyboard in your mouth
the nave of the universe
arched over your tongue
my entrance to a cluster of galaxies

Centuries old
a mantle of stars
in your eyes my birth as Venus
in a dark lagoon

On the moon -
a submerged garden
undulating tides
and breaking waves
peel the skin of my fruit

A string drawn down along my back -
Mother of Pearl
Mother of Mercy -
angels recording melodies
in the narrow between us

About the Author

Janet Hamill grew up in New Milford, New Jersey. She attended Glassboro State College in south Jersey, where she earned her baccalaureate in English. After graduation, she made New York City her base, interweaving jobs in bookstores with travels across the U.S.A. and down into Mexico. She took a freighter across the Atlantic and travelled through southern Europe, Morocco, Egypt, Sudan, Ethiopia, Kenya, and Tanzania. Upon her return, her first book of poetry was published in 1975. *Troublante* was followed by *The Temple*, *Nostalgia of the Infinite*, and *Lost Ceilings*. Her work has appeared in many journals and anthologies, and she has read widely at venues and festivals in the U.S., England and Ireland. A strong proponent of the spoken word, she has released two CDs of poetry and music—*Flying Nowhere* and *Genie of the Alphabet*. Janet's poetry evokes a sensual world where the magical and spiritual merge in a transport of dream and experience. She now resides in New York's Hudson River Valley.

This book was typeset in 11 point Garamond.
The initial print run of this book included twenty-six copies
lettered and signed by Janet Hamill and Patti Smith.

www.ingramcontent.com/pod-product-compliance
Lightning Source LLC
Chambersburg PA
CBHW021020090426
42738CB00007B/839